# How do I feel about

# BEING ANGRY

Julie Johnson

**Franklin Watts** London · Sydney

An Aladdin Book
© Aladdin Books Ltd 1999

Designed and produced by
Aladdin Books Ltd
28 Percy Street
London
W1P 0LD

First published in Great Britain
in 1999 by Franklin Watts
96 Leonard Street
London
EC2A 4RH

Designer        Gary Edgar-Hyde
Editor          Sarah Levete
Illustrator     Christopher O'Neill
Photographer    Roger Vlitos

ISBN: 0 7496 3181 3

A catalogue record for this book is
available from the British Library.

The author, Julie Johnson, is an
independent PSHE consultant
working in primary and
secondary schools.

# Contents

# Introduction

Connor, Jason, Leah, Marsha and Sim live on the same street. They are good friends. They all know what it is like to feel angry or what it is like when others get angry with them. Join them as they share their feelings about being angry and how they deal with it.

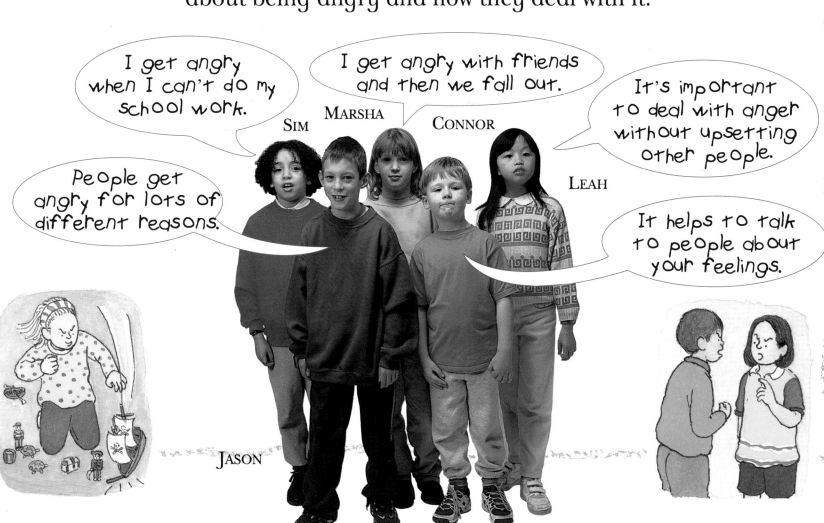

SIM: I get angry when I can't do my school work.

MARSHA: I get angry with friends and then we fall out.

LEAH: It's important to deal with anger without upsetting other people.

JASON: People get angry for lots of different reasons.

CONNOR: It helps to talk to people about your feelings.

# What is Anger?

After school, Connor is telling Leah he's been cross all day because his little brother took his favourite game without asking. Connor felt so angry he shouted at his brother and made him cry. Anger is a feeling which can last a short time or a long time. It can make you behave in different ways.

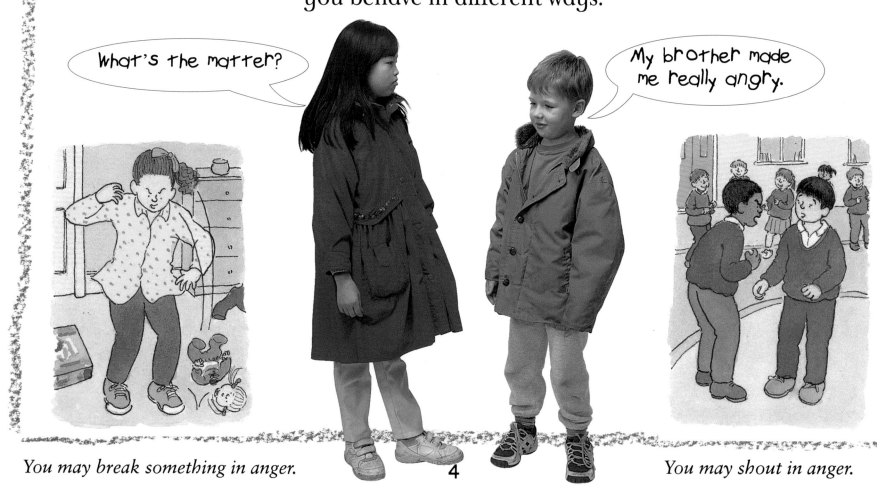

What's the matter?

My brother made me really angry.

*You may break something in anger.*

4

*You may shout in anger.*

## ▼ *Anger Is A Feeling*

Anger is a feeling, like fear or sadness. If you are having a good day and something happens to make you angry, the anger may disappear quickly.

If lots of things have upset you the anger may last for a long time. It can rumble away inside you, waiting to burst out.

## ◀ *It Can Be Sudden*

People get angry about all sorts of things and for lots of different reasons. Their anger may burst out suddenly, without any warning. Anger can make people say or do mean things.

### *Leah, what does being angry mean to you?*

"Being angry is when you are so cross you say mean things. It can make you want to break something or hurt someone.

Being angry can make you want to cry with crossness because you don't know what else to do."

5

# Being Angry With People

Marsha and Leah are best friends, but they have had an argument.

They are so angry that they aren't speaking to each other.

Can you remember when you last got angry with someone?

Who were you angry with?

Can you remember what you were angry about?

*You may get angry at school or...*

6

*... you may get angry at home.*

# Being Angry With People

1. Simon was waiting for Paulo to come round.

2. Simon rang to find out where Paulo was.

3. Paulo had arranged to do something else. Simon threw down his toy.

## Why was Simon angry?

Paulo let Simon down. He didn't even say sorry. Simon's feelings were hurt.

Instead of breaking his toy, it would have been better if Simon had told Paulo how he felt. Then Paulo may have realised how thoughtless he had been. Simon could have talked to his dad about how upset he felt.

## ▼ Best Friends

Even your best friends can make you angry. It may be something they do or say. You may see things differently from one another.

You may say, or even do, something unkind. That will only make the situation worse. It won't make you feel better.

*Oh, I took that book to school.*

## ◀ Brothers And Sisters

If you have a brother or sister, do you get angry with him or her? Perhaps he or she borrowed something without asking? Try to explain how you feel – although your brother or sister may not listen to you. If you feel very angry, talk to your parents.

## ▶ Why Not?

There will be times when a teacher or parent won't allow you to do something. Sulking, shouting or crashing around won't change their mind. Try to explain why you feel angry. Give them time to explain their reasons.

*You can't go round to Sam's today.*

### ▼ *It's All Her Fault!*

When someone has let you down, it can make you feel very angry. You may want to shout at the person you are cross with. But being angry won't change the situation. Try to remember that the person may be feeling bad anyway.

### ◀ *It Was A Mistake!*

Some people get angry very easily, when there is not much to be angry about. Without thinking, they may hit out with words, or even physically, at someone who they think has wronged them. If you do this, it is important to say sorry.

### *Marsha is angry because*...

"I told Leah a secret and she told someone else. That wasn't fair."

### *Leah is angry because*...

"I didn't think Marsha would mind. Then I got angry because Marsha said some really mean things to me."

# Being Angry With Yourself

In the playground, Jason is talking to Sim who was sent out of class for losing his temper and hitting another pupil. Sim got angry because he he was having difficulty reading a book. Have you ever got angry with yourself? Did you take your angry feelings out on yourself or out on someone else?

1. Sabrina was building a matchstick model of a house for her school project.

2. She was finding one piece really hard to fix in place.

3. Sabrina became so angry that she knocked the model over and spoilt it.

### Why was Sabrina angry?

Sabrina had been enjoying building the house. When she came to a tricky bit she lost her patience because she couldn't do it. She became frustrated and angry.

By getting angry with herself, rather than asking for some help, she stopped enjoying what she was doing. She ruined what she had been doing well up to that point.

### ▶ *Why Did I Say That?*

Sometimes people say hurtful things without thinking. They don't always realise that what they are saying is hurtful or unkind. When they think about it later, they may feel angry with themselves for having been thoughtless.

Oh, why did I say that to him? I'm so stupid.

### ▲ *I Can't Do It!*

You may get cross if you are trying to learn a new skill and find it quite difficult! You may get impatient and frustrated and want to give up.

Try to remember that it takes a while to get the hang of new things. Practice makes perfect!

### *Sim, why did you hit out?*

"I got so cross because I couldn't read. Being cross with myself made me cross with everyone else. I didn't think and I just hit another boy. It was really unfair because he hadn't done anything to upset me.

I can't always stop feeling angry, but I can stop doing or saying hurtful things."

12

# Being Angry Makes You Feel...

This morning, Connor got so angry he hit his brother, Ben. He realises he shouldn't have done this. He has hurt his brother, and his mum is now angry with him. It's important not to hit out at people, however angry you feel. It will make the situation worse – and it won't make you feel any better.

*Anger can make you feel out of control.*

13

*Anger can make you upset.*

## ▼ *Angry and Lonely*

Some people seem to be angry all the time. They take their anger out on friends. It may be that they haven't learnt to control their anger.

Friends may put up with this for a while, but may soon choose other friends.

## ◄ *Angry and Upset*

Anger can lead to lots of other feelings. You may feel frightened by your anger or it can make you feel lonely. You may feel miserable and upset because you don't understand or know what to do with your angry feelings.

Don't let Daniel play because he gets cross with you if you miss a shot.

## *Connor, how do you feel now?*

"I was wrong to hit my brother, but I wasn't wrong to feel angry. I should have told my mum how angry I felt instead of hitting Ben. Everyone feels angry, but it's what you do with your anger that can make all the problems."

14

# Hiding Other Feelings

Sim has told his teacher that he got angry because he was embarrassed and cross that he couldn't read. His teacher explained that some of us just take longer than others to learn to do something. Jason feels more settled in his new home now but at first he felt angry because he was unhappy with all the changes.

Sometimes anger can hide different feelings.

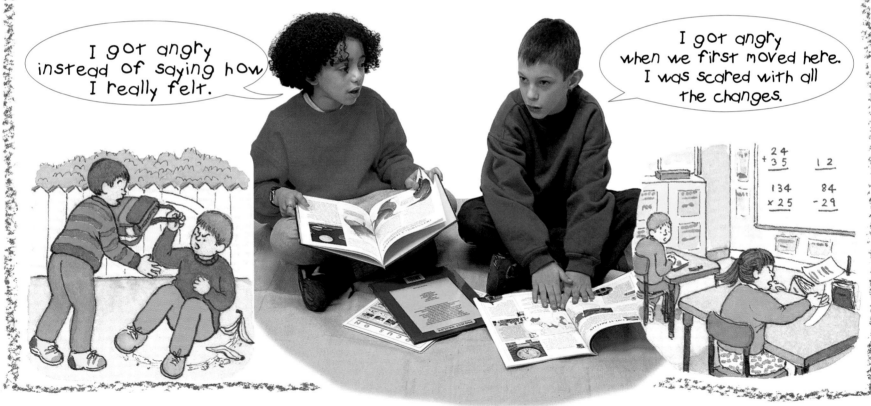

I got angry instead of saying how I really felt.

I got angry when we first moved here. I was scared with all the changes.

*Anger can hide a feeling of embarrassment.* 15 *It can hide a difficulty with learning.*

1. Adam was being bullied by a gang.

Oh, shut up. What do you know anyhow?

2. It made him angry towards his family and towards his good friends.

Adam's being bullied.

3. Adam's best friend decided to tell Adam's mum what was going on.

## Why was Adam feeling angry?

Adam was being bullied. He was frightened, confused and upset. Getting angry with the people he loved covered up these feelings.

It would have been better if Adam had told his parents or a teacher about the bullying. They would have been able to help.

## ▼ *That Doesn't Feel OK*

If someone touches you and it doesn't feel right, or if they try to make you do something you know is wrong, you may feel angry. You may feel angry if someone asks you to keep a secret which you are not happy about. If this happens, it is important to talk to a grown-up who you trust.

## ◄ *Problems At Home*

You may feel left out if a new baby arrives or you may feel confused if your parents are separating or divorcing. These feelings can make you angry. It can help to talk to a grown-up, although it may not make the situation change.

## *Jason, do you get angry easily?*

"I only recently came to this part of the country with my family. It meant lots of changes. People teased me at school because of my accent. That made me angry.

I was scared at all the new things that were happening. That made me angry, too."

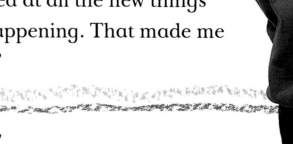

# If Someone Is Angry With You

Leah's mum gets angry with her when Leah doesn't tidy her room. Sim says his dad never used to lose his temper, but since he lost his job and is stuck at home all day, he always seems angry.

Can you remember who was last angry with you and why?

*You may not know why someone is angry...*

*... or you may know very well.*

### ▼ Saying Sorry

If a friend is angry with you because you have let him or her down, why not say sorry?

If you don't understand why a friend is angry with you, try to talk about it. Sometimes it helps to ask a grown-up to help you both talk together.

### ◀ Angry Grown-ups

Grown-ups may get cross with you because you have been naughty or have disobeyed them. Perhaps they have had a bad day at work, are not happy, or maybe someone is angry with them. Grown-ups may take their anger out on someone else, just like you can.

### Leah, what do you do when your mum is angry with you?

"If it's because I've been naughty, I say sorry and try not to do it again. If mum gets angry because she's tired or worried, I try not get upset by it. If I feel fed up about it, I talk to my grandma."

# Dealing with Angry Feelings

Marsha talked to her mum about why she was angry with Leah. Leah drew a picture of how angry and upset she felt. The next time they saw each other they were able to talk about why they were angry. Now, they have made up.

*Try writing down how you feel.*

*Try counting to ten.*

## ▼ *Put It On Paper*

Try to remember that it's when you let anger get out of control that the problems start. You can't stop feeling angry, but you can take time to think about why you may be feeling angry.

Try to write down how you feel – or paint an angry picture!

## ◄ *Ask For Help*

If you have had a very bad argument with a friend that you can't sort out, why not ask your parents to help?

If you are worried about how angry you feel, talk to a grown-up you trust. Ask him or her what they do when they get angry.

## *These are Marsha and Leah's tips for ways to deal with anger.*

"Think before you do or say anything. Think about what is making you angry. Explain calmly how you feel. Punch a pillow or take a deep breath. Try not to take your anger out on others. If you do, be prepared to say sorry."

# Don't Forget...

### Sim, how is your reading?

"Now that I don't get so angry it's a bit easier. It's still hard not to blow up, but I try to count to ten before I try a difficult word again. You can't stop angry feelings, but you can stop yourself from being unkind or hurtful to other people. It's important to talk to someone about what is making you angry."

### Leah, what do you do when your mum is angry?

"Sometimes it makes me angry that she is angry with me, when I haven't even done anything wrong! Then I tell my grandma how I feel and that helps me to understand that my mum still loves me – even when she's cross."

### Connor, do you still get angry with your brother?

"I'm going to work out how to share some of my things with my younger brother but I'm going to make sure he can't reach things which I really don't want him to borrow."

### Marsha, how do you cope with anger?

"Anger is a very strong feeling. It can come on you very quickly. But you can learn to use it and be in control of it. It's not always easy and it takes time to learn."

### Jason, what do you do when you are angry?

"Sometimes I go to my room and shout very loudly or punch a soft pillow. That makes me feel better!"

23

# Index

All the photographs in this book have been posed by models. The publishers would like to thank them all.